Standing
in the Gap

Standing in the Gap

Understanding Intercession

Johannes Facius

Sovereign World

Sovereign World Ltd
PO Box 777
Tonbridge
Kent TN11 0ZS
England

First Printing 1993
Reprinted 1998
This revised edition 2006
Originally published as *Explaining Intercession*

Scripture quotations, unless otherwise indicated, are taken from The HOLY
BIBLE, NEW INTERNATIONAL VERSION. Copyright © 1973, 1978, 1984
by International Bible Society. Used by permission of Hodder and Stoughton
Limited, a member of Hodder Headline Ltd. All rights reserved. UK
trademark number 1448790.

ISBN 1 85240 438 8

The publishers aim to produce books which will help to extend and build up
the Kingdom of God. We do not necessarily agree with every view expressed
by the author, or with every interpretation of Scripture expressed. We expect
readers to make their judgments in the light of their own understanding of
God's Word and in an attitude of Christian love and fellowship.

Typeset by CRB Associates, Reepham Norfolk
Printed in the United States of America

Notes for Study Leaders

Intercessory prayer is a vital part of the work of the Church today. Through this type of prayer, we "stand in the gap" between Almighty God and the people and nations who desperately need His mercy.

If you are studying the book as part of a group, encourage group members to read one chapter prior to each meeting and to think about the issues in advance. It can be helpful to review the content of a particular chapter at the meeting, however, to refresh everyone's memory and so that those who have not managed to do the reading will not feel embarrassed.

Five study questions at the end of each chapter are designed to stimulate discussion and prompt each person to consider how they may respond personally to the topic. Do pray together, asking for God's help to take hold of the truths presented.

May God bless you as you learn about intercession yourself and lead others in doing so.

Contents

What it Means to Stand in the Gap

I believe that intercession is the most needed ministry in the world today. Only intercession has the capacity to turn around a whole nation and change its ultimate destiny. It involves personal risk and sacrifice, and it means taking a position before God on behalf of those for whom we pray. This is what we call "standing in the gap."

A twenty-four-hour position

Let us first of all examine what "intercession" really is. Although many believers would assume that intercession is the same as prayer, in the Bible the two words are used distinctly. In 1 Timothy 2, Paul mentions *"requests, prayers, intercession and thanksgiving"* as four separate disciplines, indicating that there is a difference between prayer and intercession.

The English word "intercession" actually means, "to go in between". It can describe how a person may deliberately intervene between two parties in a situation of conflict. The word "prayer," in fact, is not directly implied in this use of the word.

Intercession is a position we take before God in a particular situation and for a specific cause. People may casually say that they were at church doing intercession for two hours on Wednesday evening, meaning that they were praying for a couple of hours. Yet true intercession cannot just be practised for a couple of hours. It is an ongoing commitment to remain in a position before God until a particular case has been solved.

In other words, intercession is a twenty-four hour position. Therefore, the intercessor is constantly before God, even if he is not actually praying for more than a small part of the time. And the power of taking such a position is very great.

I am personally very stirred by the example of Martin Luther. In 1523, the great reformer was challenged before the Catholic Church Council and the German princes to withdraw the ninety-five theses that he had so boldly nailed to the door of Worms Cathedral.

In the ground right in front of the church, a memorial stone carries this inscription: "Here stood Martin Luther and he said: 'Here I stand, I cannot do otherwise. God help me. Amen.'"

I was so deeply moved when I visited this place that I actually took off my shoes and placed myself on the stone, crying out: "God, make me into a man who can take a position and stick to it!"

Martin Luther interceded all those years ago between the erring Church and God, and his bold position not only changed his own life, it changed the world forever. God is looking for men and women who are willing to take up a position in the gap, so that he can work out His purposes on earth.

We see in the book of Exodus that when the people of Israel were in great trouble because of their sins, Moses did not just pray for them. He took up a position before God. Psalm 106:23 says:

> " . . . he [God] *said he would destroy them –*
> *had not Moses, his chosen one,*
> *stood in the breach before him*   ,
> *to keep his wrath from destroying them."*

Although Moses pleaded in prayer with God to forgive the people, the word "prayer" is not even mentioned here. It was not so much what Moses uttered with his mouth; it was the position he boldly took up in the "breach" – the same word translated in Ezekiel 22:30 as "gap."

Moses even dared get in the way of God when the Lord was furious against Israel and wanted to burn them up. In Exodus 32:10 the Lord effectively said to Moses, "Get out of my way!" But Moses did not move one inch. And by this position he became a wall of protection for the people against the wrath of the Lord.

When the apostle Paul talked about *"praying continually"* (1 Thessalonians 5:17), he did not expect people to be on their knees for twenty-four hours a day. Rather, we are to take a firm position before the Lord in a certain matter or for a certain group of people, even while we are about our daily work.

In Isaiah 62:6–7, the prophet speaks about the ministry of the watchman:

> *I have posted watchmen on your walls, O Jerusalem;*
> *they will never be silent day or night.*
> *You who call upon the* LORD,
> *give yourselves no rest,*

and give him no rest till he establishes Jerusalem
and makes her the praise of the earth.

These are intercessors who don't just pray occasionally for Jerusalem, but who are positioned around the clock to remind the Lord of His promises. They are before the Lord "day and night" and give Him no rest until His promises are fulfilled.

Dr Derek Prince explains in one of his books that the word "watchman" in the Hebrew can be translated as "secretary." A secretary or personal assistant knows the boss's agenda, and keeps reminding the boss about his or her appointments.

This is actually a very good picture of the work of an intercessor. We must know about God's agenda and then keep on reminding Him to do what He promised to do in His Word. We must learn to remain in a position before God until something happens concerning the issue for which we are praying. This is one of the clear characteristics of the work of intercession.

A sacrifice and a risk

The second basic feature of intercession is that it always requires a sacrifice. With ordinary prayer, we do not necessarily have to sacrifice anything, except some personal time. We can sit in a safe position while praying for people distant from us who are in a situation of danger or need.

All prayer is worthwhile and valuable, but intercession is distinct. Intercession requires sacrifice. If you want to intercede for somebody, you need to be able to spiritually identify with that person, and that will require something extra.

You might not be able to physically stand in the shoes of the person you are interceding for, but by the help of the Holy Spirit you must take upon yourself the whole situation of that person for whom you are interceding. This is what we call the principle of identification.

This is true in the lives of the great intercessors in the Bible. First and foremost, we see this in the life of the greatest intercessor ever, the Lord Jesus Himself. Both Romans 8:34 and Hebrews 7:25–27 speak about the Lord Jesus always making intercession for us before God.

This is the ministry that the Lord Jesus has held since His death, resurrection and ascension to the heavenly throne room where He is now sitting at the right-hand side of the Father. For almost two thousand years, the Lord Jesus has interceded for us, for the Church, for the people of Israel, and for the world.

This one fact underlines the great importance of the ministry of intercession. The Lord Jesus had a ministry of preaching and healing upon the earth for three and a half years, but He has now been carrying out the ministry of intercession for nearly two thousand years.

It is not only because of the prayers of Jesus on our behalf that the Father blesses us. It is because of the sacrifice of Jesus, giving His very own life for us.

This sacrifice is the factor that gives intercession its tremendous power. The Lord Jesus could have been appealing to His Father for our forgiveness and feeling sorrow for our sins while remaining in heaven forever. Yet He chose to leave glory and humble Himself as a man of suffering, finally offering up His life on the cross to atone for our sins.

It is this sacrifice that backs up Jesus' intercession before the Father. The Father is ever reminded of the fact that when Jesus is praying for us, He has already laid down His life for us and died for us, bearing all our sins.

You can imagine what impact this has on the Father's heart. How could He refuse anything that the Lord Jesus requires in prayer, while mindful of that great sacrifice that His dear Son made on our behalf?

If we look at the life of the apostle Paul, we find that the very same principle applies. In Romans, Paul is interceding for his fellow citizens the Jewish people, and he expresses his heart's desire and prayer that they may be saved (10:1). In Romans 9:1–4 he says:

> *I speak the truth in Christ – I am not lying, my conscience confirms it in the Holy Spirit – I have great sorrow and unceasing anguish in my heart. For I could wish that I myself were cursed and cut off from Christ for the sake of my brothers, those of my own race, the people of Israel.*

What a remarkable statement by Paul! He is speaking of a continual grief put into his heart by the Holy Spirit, to the point of wishing that he himself could take on a curse and be separated from Christ if it could serve any purpose for his brothers, the Israelites.

Here, Paul reveals the Spirit of the Lord Jesus Himself, being willing to die and even to be separated from God for eternity if that sacrifice could bring God's people to salvation. This is the very heart of Jesus.

Of course, Paul knows that he could not save anybody by being cut off from Christ. Only the death of the Son of God, the sinless Lamb, is able to atone for sin. Yet it is this

Christ-like spirit that gives intercession its tremendous power and underlines every prayer. Paul demonstrates the principle of intercession, being willing to make sacrifices in order for other people to come to know the truth.

We have already made reference to the great intercessor Moses, whom the Lord used to lead His people out of Egypt to the Promised Land. Four times during the journey throughout the wilderness, God became so upset with the rebellion and sin of the people that He wanted to punish and even destroy them, but because of Moses' intercession, the people were rescued and allowed to continue their journey.

Earlier we saw in Psalm 106 how Moses stood in the breach to protect the Israelites from the wrath of God. Of course, by doing so Moses was running a great risk.

In Exodus 32 we read the story: after the tragedy with the golden calf, the wrath of God burned against the Israelites. The Lord said that He would destroy the people and make another beginning with Moses. Yet Moses boldly took up a position in the gap between them, replying that he would be willing for his name to be taken out of the Book of Life if God would only spare the people. He was prepared to pay an enormous spiritual sacrifice for Israel to be saved from God's wrath.

Furthermore, Moses risked his life physically, because if God had actually carried out His threat against the people, he would have been the first one to be slain by the fire.

There is then in true intercession both a risk and a sacrifice. The heart of God was so deeply moved by Moses' willingness to lay down both his physical life and his eternal future on behalf of this rebellious people that God answered his prayer. It wasn't Moses' prayer that made the difference, though; it was his sacrifice.

This is the spirit of the cross, just as Christ gave up His own life for the benefit and the blessing of others. That is what moved the heart of God to forgive the grave sin of idolatry and permit His people to continue towards the Promised Land.

As with Paul, we see that God was not willing to accept the great offer that Moses made. First of all, it is not for anybody to suggest his name to be removed from the Book of Life. This is God's own sovereign choice. Secondly, there was and there is no need for anybody to die for the sins of others, other than the only one who was appointed to do so, namely the Lord Jesus Christ.

In intercession, even if we have the willingness, God would never accept these kinds of sacrifices because He already accepted one sacrifice for all by His own dearly beloved Son. Nevertheless there are sacrifices that God requires and that we must give in order to make our prayers heard and to call down an answer from heaven.

One very obvious sacrifice that goes along with prayer and intercession is fasting. Fasting is laying down something of our own self-life, and that will always energize and empower our prayers. That is why, in the New Testament, prayer is closely connected to fasting. Fasting in itself is not worth much more than the bodily benefit we can get from it, but it becomes a tremendous, powerful addition to our prayer life because it signifies a sacrifice given along with our intercession.

Sacrifice is a vital part of the life of intercession. When God looks down and listens to the prayers of His people, the self-denial of fasting is evidence of a great determination to have those prayers heard. His heart is moved tremendously by people willing to pay a price.

The power of fasting can even be seen in the world, as in the hunger strike of five young Irish Republican Army men in the Maze prison. Their starvation to the death turned them into great heroes among the Irish people, even reinforcing the dedication of those committed to the violent IRA cause. If hunger striking is effective for evil, how much more powerful will it be when it is done in love and faith, to save people from judgment?

Fasting from food is one way of paying a sacrifice; fasting from other time-consuming activities is another one that we must be prepared to do. Are we really willing to give up our time to God? If we want to see the Lord move in the things we long for, we need to sacrifice other things and spend time seeking His face.

We modern believers struggle to do this in our very busy age. But if we are not willing to put aside other things that are taking up our time and come before the Lord and plead our cases before Him, we will never be able to see real breakthroughs in our prayer life.

We find it hard to understand why the Lord does not seem to be in a hurry to respond to our requests. It is as if the Lord is taking His time before answering the prayers of His saints. There could be many reasons for this, but perhaps He wants to see whether we are really sincere and earnest about the things we are praying for. This is why we need to take time when we come before God.

In Exodus when the Lord called Moses up to the mountain, He told him to be ready and present himself to the Lord. Even Moses had to wait before God called him into His presence.

The Lord wants to see if we really desire the things that we are praying for so much that we are determined to persevere until we see His face. Ordinary prayers can be quickly prayed and quickly forgotten, but intercession is different. When we stand in the gap, it can be a long-term battle; it is a testing time for our determination and our sincerity of heart before the Lord. Without sacrifice, intercession will never really be effective.

Discussion questions

1. How is intercession distinct from other forms of prayer?

2. What risk did Moses take in standing in the gap between God and the people of Israel?

3. In what way is a secretary a good picture of an intercessor?

4. What does the intercessory ministry of Jesus teach us?

5. What sacrifices might God be calling you to make personally as part of your own prayer life?

The Dynamics of Intercession

Standing in the gap

I believe that intercession can accomplish things that no other Christian ministry could ever do in changing the destiny of a nation. There are two Old Testament scriptures that I would like to refer to in this connection.

In Isaiah 59 we see how the judgment of God was coming on His people because of their sin and rebellion. The prophet says:

> He [God] *saw that there was no-one,*
> *he was appalled that there was no-one to intervene;*
> *so his own arm worked salvation for him,*
> *and his own righteousness sustained him.*
>
> (Isaiah 59:16)

In other words, the Lord had expected somebody to intervene (in other words, to intercede: to come before Him and plead the people's case). Yet to His dismay there was not one single person to be found. Therefore, the Lord took action on His own and went out in righteousness and justice through Jesus Christ.

The amazing thought is that if an intercessor had been found, it would have made a difference to the way the Lord would have dealt with His people. If God had already made up His mind to punish His people, why would He be looking for an intercessor, or be surprised not to find one? It seems that He desired to prevent such severe punishment coming upon Israel.

We do not read that when God came down to judge His people, He expected to see an evangelist. It does not say that He was surprised that there was no pastor, or that He would have been grateful if there had been a prophet or an apostle. Evangelists, pastors, prophets and apostles are needed in the Church today, but intercession has a unique power to change the course of our nations.

In Genesis 18 we read that when the Lord came down to see what was happening in Sodom and Gomorrah, He first visited Abraham. He chose to stop and tell Abraham what He was about to do, so that Abraham could make intercession. Because of that, Lot and his family were removed before the fire fell from heaven and destroyed the cities. But there was much more in it than the salvation of one family.

It was not just a concern about his relatives that made Abraham intercede before God, but his desire for God to withhold His hand from destroying ten thousand inhabitants of the twin cities of Sodom and Gomorrah. We see this clearly when Abraham began his negotiations and kept challenging the Lord, saying, *"Will you sweep away the righteous with the wicked? What if there are fifty righteous people in the city?"* (Genesis 18:23–24). He then went from fifty to forty, thirty to twenty people.

Abraham's last offer was ten righteous people, and the

Lord answered, *"For the sake of ten, I will not destroy it"* (Genesis 18:32). However, as we know, there weren't even ten righteous people, and so in the end, Sodom and Gomorrah were destroyed.

Yet we see how God's heart went out to find a possible solution. We know from Scripture that he is not interested in the death of any sinner. God took the initiative to call Abraham to stand in the gap and to intercede for Sodom and Gomorrah.

Unfortunately, the terms that Abraham settled with the Lord for saving the cities could not be met. Perhaps he did not dare to ask for the cities to be saved for fewer than ten people. But the principle remains:

▶ **Intercession is required to influence God's heart to turn from judgment and bring salvation to the people of a city.**

> *"I looked for a man among them who would build up the wall and stand before me in the gap on behalf of the land so that I would not have to destroy it, but I found none. So I will pour out my wrath on them and consume them with my fiery anger, bringing down on their own heads all they have done, declares the Sovereign LORD."*
>
> (Ezekiel 22:30–31)

The picture is the same as in Isaiah 59: the people had fallen away from the Lord, sin was abounding, and the Lord could no longer tolerate what was going on. Yet even as He was moving towards His people in judgment, He was seeking someone to intercede for them. Unfortunately in this case, He found no one.

We must conclude that if a single person had been found to build a wall and stand in the gap between the Lord and the people in intercessory prayer, God would not have destroyed the land. He would have found another way of dealing with the sins of the people.

I am not saying that our intercession prevents God from judging evil, or that He will tolerate sin forever. This is not true. Nor can we talk about changing the will of God, because His will cannot be changed. But we can alter the way in which God will execute His will. He can choose to deal with the sins of a city or nation without destroying the people and the land.

God can destroy sin through revival, by bringing people on their knees to repent before Him. We know that from the story of Nineveh. Though it was facing the severe judgment of God and destined for destruction, through Jonah's message the whole city repented. From the greatest to the least, everyone turned away from their sins.

God forgave the city and spared it, and it remained for another five hundred years before a final judgment came and Nineveh was destroyed. So intercession can change the way in which God will deal with a sinful nation, opening up the way for a spiritual revival to deal with ungodliness.

Confronting the powers of darkness

The second dynamic of intercession is its ability to block the enemy's activity against the Church. In Genesis 3:15 the Lord says that the woman's offspring will crush the head of the serpent. He is speaking prophetically about the authority of the Church to deal with the devil's many schemes to attack her life and work in the Kingdom.

The Lord Jesus echoes this when speaking in Matthew 18:18–19 about binding and loosing. He says,

> *"I tell you the truth, whatever you bind on earth will be bound in heaven, and whatever you loose on earth will be loosed in heaven. Again, I tell you that if two of you on earth agree about anything you ask for, it will be done for you by my Father in heaven."*

Loosing and binding the powers of darkness is done only in the context of prayer. This is spiritual, or prayer war-fare: not a kind of magic, but a part of the ministry of intercession. It has to do with agreeing together in prayer. Through united, corporate prayer we can frustrate the powers of darkness as they try to come against the work of the Church.

This is confirmed further by another statement by the Lord Jesus in Matthew 16:18–19 as He responds to the confession of Simon Peter:

> *"And I tell you that you are Peter, and on this rock I will build my church, and the gates of Hades will not overcome it. I will give you the keys of the kingdom of heaven; whatever you bind on earth will be bound in heaven, and whatever you loose on earth will be loosed in heaven."*

As the Lord Jesus is speaking about the gates of Hell, He shows that He has given His Church authority to prevail over the powers of evil. This is by prayer ministry in the heavenly, unseen realms, rather than through confronting people. How else can we move into the spiritual world than by prayer?

So, the dynamics of intercession include the capacity to confront the powers of darkness as they seek to hinder the work of the Kingdom. And the Lord sends His divine messengers to help us in this.

Another wonderful dynamic of the ministry of intercession is that it puts into operation the angelic forces. In the very well known passage of James 5:16, the apostle says: *"The prayer of a righteous man is powerful and effective."* In another translation, this verse reads: *"The effective prayer of a righteous man stirs up much activity."*

This understanding can also be found in the Amplified New Testament, in which the scripture reads:

> *The earnest (heartfelt, continued) prayer of a righteous man makes tremendous power available – dynamic in its working.*

This means that when we move in intercessory prayer, we cause angelic forces to work on behalf of the Kingdom to accomplish the will of God.

What a comforting thought! So often we feel that as intercessors in the church we are but a small minority, whereas in fact God's praying people are always linked up with the activity of powerful angels. As we are praying, God is commanding His angels to work on our behalf.

This is quite clear when we look at the book of Daniel, chapter 10. We see that when Daniel gave himself to prayer and partial fasting, his prayer caused a battle to take place in the spiritual realm. The Scriptures say that from the first day that Daniel turned his face towards God and began to seek the Lord in prayer, God sent His angel to deliver the answer.

It so happens in this case that on the way down this angel was held up by a dark prince called the Prince of Persia. A battle took place where the messenger of God had to call back to heaven for help, and the archangel Michael then had to come to his assistance. In the end, the power of this dark Prince of Persia was overcome so that the angel could reach Daniel with God's message.

So, we are not left alone, but on the contrary are joining up with a vast host of angelic forces ready to work at God's command.

Please note that it is not biblical for us to try to address angels or command them to go here or there. On the contrary, the Bible clearly states that the angels are the servants of the Lord of hosts and they obey His commands. When we appeal to the Lord in prayer, as a consequence of our intercession, He will command His angels to work on our behalf.

Producing an outpouring of the Holy Spirit

A final aspect of intercession is that it can produce an outpouring of the Holy Spirit. Both in Acts 2, where the first outpouring of the Holy Spirit on the day of Pentecost is recorded, and Acts 4, where another outpouring of the Spirit is described, it is very clear that this was the result of intercession made by the Church.

There is today much misunderstanding as to how a revival can be brought about. Some Christians try to bring about the release of the Holy Spirit by making proclamations of faith or strong confessions, or even by directly commanding the Spirit to be released. But the New Testament shows us a different way.

First of all, we are not able to take charge over the Holy Spirit and make Him obey our commands. It is actually the other way around; it is the Spirit who is the Lord, and we are to be subject to His will and command. We are never given authority to instruct the Holy Spirit to move here and there, or to choose when He should pour out His power. The only way to see a true outpouring of the Holy Spirit is when the Church begins to engage in long-term united intercession.

The same principle is confirmed in every revival that has happened in the history of the Church. We can see that the wind of the Spirit came as a result of intercessory prayer. As we take that to heart, we will understand that today too the Church must dedicate herself to persevering prayer before the Lord of the harvest, to pour out His Spirit and send out His workers to bring in the harvest.

It is the same if we want to receive the Holy Spirit personally. Jesus said that the Lord gives good things to those who ask Him (Matthew 7:11). We cannot receive the power of the Holy Spirit by our own strength or activity. It is only by turning to the Lord and humbly seeking His face that He will grant us the power of His Spirit.

Discussion questions

1. Why does God look for someone to intervene before He brings judgment on people?

2. What does it mean to "stand in the gap"?

3. How can we rightly confront the powers of darkness?

4. What does the Bible tell us about the activity of angels in relation to intercession?

5. How can we see an outpouring of the Holy Spirit in our own lives and in the Church?

The Principle of the Body

There is a vast difference between the power of individual prayer and that of corporate prayer. We can see in the New Testament that the promises God gives to His people when they pray together "with one accord," are much greater than those given for individual praying.

In Acts 1:14 we read that the followers of Jesus *"all joined together constantly in prayer"* just before they were baptized in the Holy Spirit. Similarly in Acts 4:24, Peter and John along with their fellow believers *"raised their voices together in prayer to God,"* as they asked for boldness and miraculous signs. Verse 31 tells us,

> *After they prayed, the place where they were meeting was shaken. And they were all filled with the Holy Spirit and spoke the word of God boldly.*

These major outpourings of the Holy Spirit could never have resulted just from people praying on their own. It is when the Church begins to join together in unity and seek the Lord with one mind and soul that tremendous things can happen.

Generally speaking, because of the modern trend toward

individualism, the western Church has lost this key understanding of being a unified body. In Africa and the Far East, Christians have a much better understanding of the necessity and the value of working together. But in the West this is still largely a foreign concept.

Much of western Christianity is therefore based more on Old Testament principles, where only special members of the community could be priests and prophets. Consequently churches struggle to attain real unity and to learn to move together in the Spirit.

God's way of working in the Old Covenant was to use great individuals like the prophets, Isaiah, Jeremiah, Daniel and King David, Nehemiah and so on, to do His work. Through these faithful servants filled with God's Spirit, He was able to reveal His divine will and accomplish His purposes on the earth. But as part of the New Covenant, God's focus is no longer on great individuals. He is now seeking a body of Spirit-filled believers.

It is my deep conviction that the New Testament must be understood according to the principle of the body. The Scriptures of the New Testament are not just for individuals; they have been written for God's united people. The day of Pentecost was in its essence the birth of the Body of Christ.

Only the unified Body of Christ is able to fully express who Jesus is. No individual, however great and saintly, holy and mature he or she might be, could ever express the personality of Jesus. He is far too great, too rich and too wonderful for any single person to encompass. It takes the whole body to manifest the full nature of Christ. God desires to see His Church united so that His Son can be truly revealed to the world.

It is for that purpose that the Holy Spirit was given. The baptism of the Holy Spirit is not just to equip people to exercise charismatic gifts, or even to give them boldness to witness about Jesus. The real, deep significance of Pentecost is found in Paul's first letter to the Corinthians 12:13 where it says,

For we were all baptized by one Spirit into one body.

God poured out the Holy Spirit to form us into a body that could function in unity and love. The birth of that wonderful Body of Christ was on the day of Pentecost when this diverse group of people, by the outpouring of the Holy Spirit, was melted together into a corporate whole before God.

It was God's clear intention that we as believers under the New Covenant should live joined together as members of one another. We need to learn to move together, to work together and do all the business of our Christian ministry together.

In many churches today the members, although belonging to the same local church, are very often divided into many different factions. There might be a group that is very much taken up with the worship, another one might feel the calling to pray, and yet another might be outgoing in evangelism, and so on.

Some years ago, I talked to a church pastor who had a church of about a thousand members. I had been invited to have a prayer seminar in his church, but when I entered the church, I discovered that only a tiny group – maybe about a hundred people – had come together to participate. However, during the prayer seminar, which took place in the main church hall, I could hear the sound of people singing in another part of the church building, and a little later another group of people came out and left the church.

This made me ask the pastor at the end of our meeting what was going on, and he kindly explained to me that in his church there were thirty-six different groups engaged in so-called "expert" ministries. He added that he hardly ever saw the whole church come together in one gathering.

This is a characteristic of the way the Church is operating in the western world. Yet I do not believe that this is God's intention. He wants us to learn to do everything together. In the early Church, when there was evangelism, the whole church was engaged in evangelism. When there was worship, the whole church was worshipping. When there was prayer, all the believers came together to seek the Lord.

It is therefore true to say that the New Testament concept of Church is a corporate one. The language is "we" and not "I." We are all individually church members, but it is the body that counts before God, and which He has chosen for His service in the world. Learning this would be a great help for us as we seek to understand the real power of intercessory prayer.

It is interesting to notice that when Jesus in Matthew 18:18–20 speaks about the authority to bind and to loose, He is actually addressing the Church. He is speaking about what the Church can do, not what an individual can do. Without understanding this, we get wrong ideas about how spiritual authority can be properly exercised.

Jesus promised,

> "... *if two of you on earth agree about anything you ask for, it will be done for you by my Father in heaven.*"
>
> (Matthew 18:19)

He does not say, "If one of you is asking about anything, it shall be granted." He is stressing plurality here by using the least expression that you can have for the body, *"if two of you agree..."* This indicates that only in this corporate sense are binding and loosing possible.

How much confusion there has been in the Church in recent years over this matter! Many individuals are trying by their own individual faith and power to bind great principalities and powerful angels of darkness. This kind of authority is not meant for a solitary believer, but for the Church.

This is why the Lord Jesus says that where two or three are gathered in His name, He will manifest his presence. A single believer is very limited when it comes to manifesting the presence and power of God, but when we come together, the Lord can reveal Himself in a fuller way.

Spiritual authority in prayer is linked with the unity of believers. Long before the Church was born, the Lord Jesus put forth this principle.

In Matthew 16:18, Jesus said, *"I will build my church, and the gates of Hades will not overcome it."* Notice how the Lord foresaw the overthrow of the powers of darkness through the building of His Church. He was not giving authority to storm the gates of Hell to Peter on his own.

It is a grave misunderstanding to think that power to take on the whole hierarchy of the devil is possessed by individuals. The chosen instrument for overcoming the powers of the enemy is the whole Church. Only as the Church comes into its own will we have authority to defeat Satan's strategems.

" . . . I will build my church, and the gates of Hades will not overcome it."

(Matthew 16:18)

As believers learn to flow together in harmony, we will also begin to move in one accord in our prayer ministry. There is no other way in which we can cast the satanic power structure down from its position in the spiritual realm. The Church is central to everything that God has purposed to do in the world.

As we grow in our understanding and practice of true corporate prayer, we will come to see much more authority exercised against the powers of the enemy, and also much more fruit brought forth in the life of the Church.

The radiant bride

There is no doubt that the unity of the Church is a high priority in the heart of God. Of course God desires to answer the prayers of His dearly beloved Son, the Lord Jesus, *"that all of them may be one"* (John 17:21).

This important matter must be resolved before the Lord Jesus comes again. I do not believe that Jesus is returning to fetch a divided, miserable and spiritually poor Church. He is coming to get a glorious Bride, fully prepared for the great day of the wedding to her heavenly Bridegroom.

In the last days of this age, the Holy Spirit is working powerfully to perfect the Church. And if she is to be ready for the coming of her Head and Lord, true unity has to be established between the different parts of the Body of Christ.

Because the last days will be a very difficult time of trials and testing, some Christians think that the Church must concentrate just on surviving against the increasing pressure of satanic opposition. Although it is very true that the end times will be more challenging than any other period of the life of the Church, this perspective is not biblical.

The New Testament shows that Jesus offered up His life to get Himself a *"radiant church, without stain or wrinkle or any other blemish, but holy and blameless,"* as Ephesians 5:27 puts it. Jesus is not coming back for a divided, depressed and beaten Church. He is coming back to get a glorious Church, a Bride who has adorned herself and made herself ready for her Husband.

> *"Let us rejoice and be glad*
> *and give him glory!*
> *For the wedding of the Lamb has come,*
> *and his bride has made herself ready.*
> *Fine linen, bright and clean,*
> *was given her to wear."*
>
> (Revelation 19:7–8)

We expect that a bride prepared for her wedding would not look miserable, worn out or scattered, but would instead radiate beauty and youth. And this is the picture of the Church, a glorious Church that will stand in the last days just before the return of the Lord Jesus.

One of the essential features of this glorious Church must be unity. When Jesus in John's gospel, chapter 17 prays for the Church, His Body, he says,

> *"I have given them the glory that you gave me, that they*
> *may be one as we are one."*
>
> (John 17:22)

It is interesting to notice that Jesus connects glory with unity. He says that He gave the glory He received from His Father to His disciples in order to make them one. That means that whenever the Church is flowing in unity, she reflects the glory of the Lord Jesus. On the other hand, if there is no unity in the Body of Christ, then there is no glory either, no matter how much we try to proclaim it to be so.

In that light, a glorious Church means a body of believers flowing in love for one another. So, if Jesus is to return soon, the unity of the Church becomes perhaps the highest priority for intercessory prayer.

The Lord Jesus Himself devoted His last high priestly prayer on earth to that cause, and we can be sure that this is a major burden upon God's heart today. Consequently the Holy Spirit is stirring the hearts of believers all over the world to pray for the oneness of the Church.

As we follow that prompting, we will enjoy the presence of the Holy Spirit. It has been my joy to see on my many travels around the world that whenever people are flowing with God's purposes, they come under the special anointing of the Spirit. I have witnessed how churches devoting themselves to praying for the unity of local believers experience great blessings and spiritual growth.

This is what happened in my own church back in Denmark. The Lord began to teach us that He did not want us to make our own church affairs the foremost priority for our prayer ministry. As the pastor, I instructed the people to always remember this principle, "Pray for somebody else's church before you pray for your own."

In this way, the Lord led us to pray regularly for the other churches in our area of Copenhagen, and that one factor caused much blessing to come upon us. In the course of four years, our little church grew from eighty members to about three hundred, though without any special focus on evangelism.

So let us represent the Body of Christ in all its fullness, and so prepare the Church as a glorious Bride before the Lord Jesus comes again.

Discussion questions

1. What prevents us from working together in unity as the Church?

2. How does the Old Covenant differ from the New Covenant in terms of Christian ministry?

3. Why can't we fulfil the promises of God as isolated individuals?

4. How is the Body of Christ central to God's purposes for the world?

5. What kind of Church is the Lord Jesus returning for?

Prophetic Intercession

Living according to New Testament principles means that we need to come under the direction and guidance of the Holy Spirit.

This principle applies, of course, to all aspects of Christian living, but it particularly applies to the prayer life of the believer. Our intercession should not be principally directed by circumstances or needs. Instead, it should be under the guidance of the Holy Spirit, so that we submit to His will and His way.

In John 3:8, Jesus outlines what it means to live by the Spirit. He says:

> *"The wind blows wherever it pleases. You hear its sound, but you cannot tell where it comes from or where it is going. So it is with everyone born of the Spirit."*

A New Testament Christian is not supposed to be led by external rules or regulations. Instead each one of us needs to learn to hear and obey the voice of the Holy Spirit. This means that we cannot base our prayers on our own understanding, common sense, or the available information.

We need to learn how to wait upon God and to be ready to move with Him.

So often we are controlled by our own thoughts, perhaps by our traditions and the theology in which we were brought up. But Jesus tells us that naturally speaking, we cannot know where the Spirit comes from or where He goes; we have to become spiritually sensitive to His voice. This involves being very flexible, especially when we seek God in prayer.

We need to be able to put aside all preconceived ideas, even the vital prayer subjects that we have come up with on our own, to listen to what the Holy Spirit is saying and learn what He is calling us to pray for. Only in this way can we hope to be really effective in what we are doing as intercessors.

To learn how to really exercise the ministry of inter-cession will require our complete dependency on the Holy Spirit. His role is crucial if we aim at getting through and touching God in our prayers.

In Hebrews 8:11, the writer makes a very remarkable statement about the New Covenant, quoting a prophecy from Jeremiah 31. He says:

> *"No longer will a man teach his neighbour,*
> *   or a man his brother, saying, 'Know the Lord,'*
> *because they will all know me,*
> *   from the least of them to the greatest."*

Of course Christians still need instruction. But anybody who is instructing another believer must be aware that his mission is not to take the place of the Holy Spirit in that person's life. Instead, through our teaching we are actually to push the believer closer and closer into recognizing the Spirit's inner guidance.

This is the essence of the New Covenant: every believer can know the Lord himself, and everyone can hear His voice. Our job, if we are teachers of the Word of God, is not to try and convince others about our particular theology, but enable them to find their own way to listen to the Lord.

One of the absolute basics of true intercession is therefore learning to hear the voice of God. Simply speaking, that is what we understand by prophetic prayer.

Prophecy means to sense what the Lord is saying to us now. It is not so much knowing the future or explaining eschatological truth about the end times, as interpreting what is in the heart of God for the very moment. Therefore prophetic prayer means that we seek to discern the burdens of Christ in order that we might join with Him in our prayers.

Paul speaks about the role of the Holy Spirit in the prayer life of the Church in Romans 8:26–27:

X *... the Spirit helps us in our weakness. We do not know what we ought to pray for, but the Spirit himself intercedes for us with groans that words cannot express. And he who searches our hearts knows the mind of the Spirit, because the Spirit intercedes for the saints in accordance with God's will.* X

We learn from these verses that the role of the Spirit in the life of intercession cannot be underestimated. Actually, if we are not praying and interceding by the Spirit, we are just performing the works of the flesh, which accomplish nothing.

Notice that Paul says, *"We do not know what we ought to pray for."* This is actually a fundamental truth of our prayer life. We cannot figure out the right way of praying for certain things or persons by our natural mind. Only as we come in touch with the Holy Spirit will we be able to discern the issues properly. Truly, we don't know how to pray, but *"the Spirit helps us in our weakness."*

For those of us who feel weak when it comes to prayer, there is good news. The life of prayer and intercession is for people who know their own weakness and their dependency on the help of the Holy Spirit. Those who think they are able to do things by their own intelligence and strength are simply not qualified for the life of prayer.

The fact is, our own understanding is insufficient when we are praying. We need revelation and direction from God. The Holy Spirit is the one who knows the will of God in every circumstance and in every situation for which we might be interceding. He searches hearts and He is able to discern the truth in each and every case.

However important I might think my prayer subjects might be, they must be submitted to God's leading. Intercession is when we allow ourselves to be instruments through which the Spirit can actually pray within us according to the will of God. When this happens, the burden of the Holy Spirit can be felt so strongly that we may not even be able to utter any words.

Many believers believe that prayer is the ability to express a lot of words to God. But this is far from being the truth. Prayer is the manifestation of the Holy Spirit within our innermost being, which can be something so heavy that it can only be expressed by an inward groaning.

As we come together to pray as a body of believers, we need to exercise much sensitivity to discern the burdens of the Holy Spirit. Otherwise we might just waste our time doing our own thing. We need to be open to things that have not come up naturally in our own minds. We must make ourselves available before the Lord so that we can begin to sense the burdens that are on His heart.

Let me give you a practical example of prophetic prayer. Many years ago in my local church in Copenhagen, the Lord was teaching us this matter of being sensitive to the voice of the Holy Spirit. Normally as the pastor, I would always prepare very thoroughly with a list of important issues that I felt we needed to pray through. One evening I went to the prayer meeting with my usual topics ready to share with the church, but then something unusual happened.

At that time we had learned that before we started to pray, we needed to wait upon the Lord in silent worship and adoration. As we were spending that time before God, all of a sudden one of our sisters began to weep and cry and come under the power of the Spirit. She then began to prophesy and issue a strong call to our church to pray for our brothers and sisters in China.

Normally I would be sceptical about taking guidance from a prophecy, but that evening I was convinced that it was the Holy Spirit. I have never seen a woman come under the burden of the Spirit in that way – it was just as if she was in birth pangs, trembling in pain.

At that time our church never normally thought about praying for the church in China. We had just come together to pray for Denmark as we usually did once a week. But the call of the Spirit was so strong that we had to put aside all our well-intentioned prayer issues and give ourselves to crying out to the Lord for our suffering Chinese brothers and sisters.

We actually poured out our prayers non-stop for more than three hours, interceding for people we did not even know. Purely from the burden of the Holy Spirit we were able to pray with tremendous power and conviction. This is what we understand by prophetic prayer.

Of course, to be able to flow with the Holy Spirit also means having an understanding of what God is doing in the world in our day. God is doing specific things today, distinct from those He did in previous generations. It is therefore of the utmost importance that we as believers come to understand how God is currently at work among the nations, in our own nation, and in the Church, in order that we might be prophetic in our praying.

The whole point of intercession is to work together with God for the fulfilment of His purposes in the world. And how can we do that if we don't have a clue about what God is doing in our present-day situation?

We have already talked of the unity of the Body of Christ as a vital area of prayer in these last days. Let me suggest to you two other major things that I believe that the Holy Spirit is doing right now in the world.

Preaching to all nations

First of all, I am convinced that we are living in those days foretold by the Scriptures when the Great Commission shall be fulfilled and the gospel taken to the ends of the earth. In Matthew 24:14, Jesus says:

"And this gospel of the kingdom will be preached in the whole world as a testimony to all nations, and then the end will come."

We must understand that a key area of the Holy Spirit's work is to bring the message of the Lord Jesus Christ to all the people groups, tongues and tribes who have not yet heard about the salvation of God.

Therefore this area becomes a focus of our intercessions. If we give ourselves to that which is God's priority on the earth, then, of course, we will begin entering into the anointing of the Holy Spirit. The secret of successful intercession is to be concerned with things that God considers important, and which He is working on today among the nations.

World evangelism today is a major area for intercessors to take on. But we have to understand it rightly. It is not a matter of preaching the gospel to the same people over and over again, but to the furthest ends of the earth.

If the Church is only evangelizing the same areas over and over again, we are not really obeying Christ. The Lord said that He wanted us to testify to Him in each and every nation, and since there are still several thousand people groups in the world who have not even heard the name of Jesus, we still have a lot of work to bring to completion. So our priority must be to pray for the gospel to break through to all unreached peoples.

Among intercessors in the world today, this point has been strongly highlighted by the Holy Spirit. There are now prayer movements specifically raising up prayer for all these unreached people groups. Also, many individual churches are adopting an unreached tribe to pray and intercede for, as well as sending missionaries to them with the gospel.

I have visited churches that have taken up the burden to pray for unreached people groups, and the result has been a tremendous blessing by God. Without any special evangelistic effort on their part, the church has grown in numbers. I am not saying that we do not need to preach the gospel. We do. But an even more effective way to grow is discovering the prophetic issues that the Holy Spirit is highlighting today.

The restoration of Israel

Another key area of prophetic prayer today is to do with the restoration of Israel. It is quite evident that the Holy Spirit is working to bring back the Jewish people to their ancient land, to prepare Israel for her Messiah and for the role she will play in the coming age of the Kingdom of God.

Unfortunately, quite a few Christians have little understanding or vision for God's dealings with the Jewish people. Yet in Acts 3:21, we read that Jesus *"must remain in heaven until the time comes for God to restore everything, as he promised long ago through his holy prophets."*

In other words, the coming of the Lord Jesus is linked to the fulfilment of the prophetic scriptures about Israel. It is amazing to see today how these ancient prophecies are being fulfilled, one after another.

Intercessors are called to pray earnestly for the fulfilment of every word spoken by God through the mouth of these holy prophets. This was how it was with Daniel. When he discovered while reading Jeremiah that the time for the end of the Babylonian captivity had come, he gave himself to intercession and fasting for twenty-one days in order to pave the way for this prophecy to be fulfilled.

Real intercession is nothing but working together with God for the realization of everything that He has already foretold in His Word.

So much of what has already been fulfilled was foretold hundreds of years before. Isn't it remarkable that the prophet Micah prophesied the birth of the Messiah in the town of Bethlehem and five hundred years later, Jesus was born in Bethlehem? It would not be so amazing if the prophecy had been about one of the major cities of the ancient world. But the fact that it was such a little village as Bethlehem is an incredible testimony to the accuracy and truthfulness of God's Word.

In Isaiah 53, the prophet speaks with great accuracy about the sufferings of the coming Messiah on the cross. Virtually everyone in the evangelical church would agree that this is true. Yet when it comes to the prophecies about the people of Israel, and the return of the Jews to their homeland, there is suddenly much less unanimity. Many leading Christians spiritualize these prophecies to the extent of claiming that they pertain only to the Church.

How is it that the prophecies about Jesus' birth and His sufferings later on the cross of Calvary are understood literally, whereas the prophecies concerning the Jewish people and the restoration of Israel happening before the return of the Messiah are not?

The Church has never been dispersed to the ends of the earth and there is no homeland that all Christians ought to return to. The Lord has clearly said that Jesus will be held back in heaven until all these prophecies are fulfilled. Israel is being restored, the Jewish people are now returning by

their thousands, and God will fulfil every word He spoke
about His ancient people.

Clearly this is something that the Holy Spirit is working
powerfully to bring about in the world today. And if we
want to be in the flow of God's purposes, then we need to
join in prayer and intercession on this issue.

We have already seen how the Church is blessed when
she takes up the burdens of the Holy Spirit. Some churches
that have started to pray for Israel regularly, and like
Daniel, are calling upon the Lord to fulfil His promises to
the Jewish people, have entered into increased power of the
Spirit. It is as if the anointing that comes from praying
prophetically is spilling over, as it were, to other areas of the
work of the Church.

As we recognize where the wind is blowing and become
obedient to the Holy Spirit, there is a force operating in our
lives enabling us to be successful in almost anything that we
are doing for the Kingdom.

Discussion questions

1. What does it mean to live by the Spirit?

2. How can we learn how to pray prophetically?

3. Which major issues are on the heart of God for the world today?

4. How can we fulfil the Great Commission effectively?

5. How do you understand the prophecies in Scripture concerning Israel?

Being Available

When it comes to interceding powerfully, the main obstacles stem from lack of preparation and failure to enter into the presence of the Lord. Often we are praying the wrong way, we are stuck in our own thoughts, and we have difficulties getting in touch with the Holy Spirit as we enter into intercession.

The biggest obstacle to prayer can be the process of unloading our own thoughts, including all our burdens of anxieties and needs. This must happen before we can come to the place where we are truly available for the Holy Spirit to give us prayers according to the will of God.

If we really want to touch the Lord in our intercession, there is a certain matter that we need to pay attention to. In Romans 12:1–3, the apostle Paul points out the basis of all true ministry.

> *I urge you, brothers, in view of God's mercy, to offer your bodies as living sacrifices, holy and pleasing to God – this is your spiritual act of worship. Do not conform any longer to the pattern of this world, but be transformed by the renewing of your mind. Then you will be able to test and approve what God's will is – his good, pleasing and perfect*

will. For by the grace given me I say to every one of you: Do
not think of yourself more highly than you ought, but rather
think of yourself with sober judgment, in accordance with
the measure of faith God has given you.

It has been a great privilege in my life to know a very
great servant of the Lord, who is now with the Lord. This
man was Peter van Woerden, the nephew of Corrie ten
Boom, whose family took care of so many Jewish people
and hid them from the Nazis during the Second World
War.

I came to know Peter some years ago, and we became
very close friends, perhaps in a special way because we both
suffered from heart problems. Peter was a unique man. He
was able so often in a simple manner to put his finger on the
essential things.

The Lord healed me in 1989 and I met Peter later the
same year. Before my illness I had been involved in seven
different ministries, but at that point I had only one left,
that of being the international coordinator of Intercessors
International. I had just had a new business card printed,
and so during my brief talk with Peter, I handed him one so
he might have our new address and telephone number in
Germany.

Peter looked at the card and then remarked, "Johannes,
it says here that you are the international coordinator of the
prayer movement. You can't really be that, only the Holy
Spirit can coordinate the world prayer movement!"

I couldn't help but smile at the truth of his comment and
said, "Well, Peter, I guess you are right. But you know, this
is about the last piece of ministry that I have, so if you take
this away from me, I have absolutely nothing left."

We both laughed and I then asked him curiously what ministry he was involved with. At first he looked a little surprised, then he said, "If I told you the kind of ministry I have, I am not sure you would believe me." I replied that I would like to know anyway, and then came his unique answer, "I have the ministry of availability!"

I said to Peter, "I haven't heard about that ministry before. You'd better tell me what that is," and so he gave me an example of what it means to be available for God.

Years ago, when he and his wife went to Jerusalem to get a flat to live in part-time for their ministry, the Lord led them to a small house in the Christian quarter of the Old City in Jerusalem. As they moved in, they asked the Lord to show them what kind of church they should be attending. Peter had hoped that they would become part of the more lively, evangelical churches in Jerusalem, but the Lord had something different in mind and answered very clearly that they should attend the services in the small, Syrian Orthodox church that was right below their flat. They were very surprised.

First of all, they had not even noticed the church before, and secondly, they had no idea of how to worship in a Syrian Orthodox church. However, they decided to obey the Lord and started going to that little church. They did not understand what the priest was saying or doing as he ministered before the altar, and they were the only people that ever attended the church. So they decided to intercede and pray for the priest during the services.

A couple of months went by, during which they came regularly to worship the Lord and pray in that little church. But one Sunday Peter was sick and unable to go, so his wife decided to stay home to care for him. As they returned the following Sunday, the priest came down for the first time after the service to talk to them. He looked very bleak as he asked them, "Where were you last Sunday? You are not going to leave me, are you?"

Then Peter said to his wife, "Let us put our hands upon this man and pray for him," and as they did this, the Holy Spirit came upon this Syrian Orthodox priest. He was met by God, became filled with the Spirit and was born again as a completely different person.

This is what can happen when we become completely available to the Holy Spirit. It is also what Paul speaks of as the very foundation of any ministry in the Body of Christ. We are to present our bodies as living sacrifices and put them on the altar before God. Because when you are laid on the altar, you become available for God.

In Old Testament days when people sacrificed animals on the altar, they had to bind them to the horns of the altar to prevent them from jumping off at the first opportunity. Once we lay ourselves on the Lord's altar, we can no longer do our own thing or go our own way. We have to lie there silently, waiting for God to act.

Paul says that we should not be conformed to this world, but be transformed by the renewing of our minds so that we may be able to understand God's will. And this is exactly what we are talking about here. As we come to pray, our greatest need is to be delivered from defiling thoughts and motives and be renewed in our minds so that we can discern the will of the Lord. Only when we have laid all things down as we wait on God, will we have reached the place where true intercession can begin.

When Paul and his co-workers were praying in Antioch as recorded in Acts 13:1–3, we read that they were worshipping the Lord and fasting. This means that they were simply seeking the face of the Lord; they did not have any specific subject for their prayers. It was during this time that they entered into the presence of the Lord and the Holy Spirit called Paul and Barnabas to become the first missionaries to Europe.

I am convinced that when Paul and the other apostles and servants of the Lord met that day, they were not there to discuss how they could best bring the gospel to Europe. I don't even think it was in their minds. But they were taken up with a desire to seek the Lord, to worship Him, and to be ready for whatever purpose He might have for them. It was out of that availability that the gospel came to the European continent for the first time.

Some years ago, a pastor from Norway sought my advice on a problem in his prayer life. Every time he would come before the Lord, he felt bombarded by preoccupations: what he was supposed to speak on in the next morning's service; what needed to be written in the next church bulletin; where to get the money to pay the bills; and all the various needs of his family and ministry. And before long, he would be so frustrated that he would actually give up praying.

When I listened to him, it struck me that this pastor did not really understand the nature of true prayer. I told him that prayer is not bringing to God all the things that we think are important, but instead being available to listen to whatever He wants to say to us. If we cannot learn to unwind our busy minds and put down every anxious thought, we will never come to the place where the Holy Spirit can begin to inspire us and help us in prayer.

We need to have our minds renewed. We need to know what it is to empty ourselves before God and just come to the point where we can say with the prophet, "Lord, here I am." We are only instruments and vessels for the Holy Spirit. We don't need to initiate the process of prayer; that part belongs to God.

In John 15:16, the Lord Jesus says to the disciples:

> *"You did not choose me, but I chose you and appointed you to go and bear fruit – fruit that will last. Then the Father will give you whatever you ask in my name."*

It might seem unnecessary for the Lord to say that we did not choose Him, but that He chose us. Yet we need this to be underlined because many of us often act as if we had actually chosen God for our own purposes and needs, instead of realizing that He is the one who has chosen us for His purposes and for His needs.

Jesus says that He appointed us to go and bear lasting fruit, so that whatever we ask the Father in His name would be given to us. We can only bear fruit as we dwell in Him. This is an important principle that applies to intercession.

The success of our prayer depends on whether the things we are interceding for are of God's choosing, or whether they are of our own choice, emotions, or burdens. If we try to get the Lord to go along with what we feel is important, we are actually dictating to Him. But when we are in the area of His appointment, our intercessory ministry will bear fruit that lasts for eternity.

This is the secret of the amazing promise that, *"The Father will give you whatever you ask in my name."* If we do not understand the context, we can easily be deceived into thinking that the Lord will give us whatever we might feel like asking Him. That is not what the Word tells us. It is when we are immersed in His life that we will receive answers to our prayers.

With intercession, we cannot just plunge into everything that catches our interest, or even that other people think that we need to intercede for. The Lord Jesus has appointed us to certain areas of ministry and we need to remain within His appointment. Then whatever we ask His Father will be given to us.

This is why we need to come before the Lord and make ourselves available for that which is of Him. We need to be transformed from the corruption of this world and be renewed in our minds so that we can discern the good, acceptable, and perfect will of God.

A very well-known intercessor said to me many years ago, "The most important thing about prayer is to make sure that you are coming into the presence of the Lord, and from there the Holy Spirit will lead you and give you His burden." He went on, "If you have ten minutes available to pray, then use the first eight minutes to be still and empty yourself before God and worship Him. Then the remaining two minutes in intercessory prayer will be tremendously effective."

We need to understand that nothing with our God is by accident. Everything goes according to His preordained plan. In Ephesians 2:8 Paul says:

> *It is by grace you have been saved, through faith – and this is not from yourselves, it is the gift of God.*

Then in verse 10 he continues:

*For we are God's workmanship, created in Christ Jesus to
do good works, which God prepared in advance for us to do.*

The amazing thing about our salvation is that God has
redeemed our lives for His purposes. He has prepared us
in Christ Jesus for good works that were ordained before
the foundation of the world. The scripture tells us that
God not only chose us to become His children, but He
also planned the very details of what we are supposed
to do.

Just think about it: every day God has prepared the
people that we are going to meet, the actions that we
should take, the decisions that we need to make. All of that
is not just happening by coincidence. It is a well prepared
plan that God long ago devised for our lives, as we truly
follow Him.

The vital thing for us then is to discover God's plan, and
to do that we must be available. We need to come before
the Lord to find out what He has planned for us for each
and every day. And it is precisely the same with intercession. We must come to the point where we can discern
God's plan for our prayer time together. To do this we need
to trust that God has already prepared beforehand what we
are to do, say and pray.

In my earlier days in the ministry, I always used to
prepare carefully for everything that I was going to be a part
of. I inherited from my father a logical, systematic German
mind, and went to great effort to have everything under
control at each occasion. Of course, it's not necessarily
wrong to prepare or to work systematically, but all of that
can become an enemy of listening to the Spirit and grasping
the burden of God's heart for the moment.

Before my illness, I was one of the most thorough and hard-working Bible teachers you could imagine. I led seven Christian ministries, but when I was put through the fire with three years of non-stop pain and depression, I lost all of them. However, when the Lord healed me on that Saturday morning in February in 1989, I fully expected that He would restore all of these leadership responsibilities and even add some more to the list.

As I was seeking the Lord for my future, however, He clearly said to me that He was not going to give me back these seven ministries. Instead, He told me not to worry about what to do for Him or engage myself in endless activity to serve Him. This was not necessary. Through Ephesians 2:10 He showed me that His own plan for me had been thought out and well planned even before the foundation of the world.

The Lord told me that He wanted me in my new resurrection life to simply discover day by day what He had prepared for me. I was to do only the things that He would quicken my heart to do, and go only to the places that He would give me a burden for. I was no longer to try to organize my own ministry.

I was to become completely available for Him, in readiness to go wherever He wanted to send me and to do exactly what was on His heart. And I have found that such a position before God is the best foundation for an effective intercessory ministry.

Discussion questions

1. What are the greatest obstacles to listening to the Holy Spirit?

2. How would you describe the "ministry of availability"?

3. What is the best way to come to a time of prayer?

4. Why is it significant that Jesus has chosen us and appointed us to bear fruit?

5. Are you available to go where God is leading you?

Confidence and Trust

Intercession cannot be learned through manuals or methods. Intercession is a ministry that flows out of our very relationship with God. One key area of this relationship is our ability to trust in the Lord.

Generally speaking, prayer is rather pointless unless we believe. Time after time, the New Testament writers emphasize that when we pray we must believe that we are being heard by our Father in heaven, and believe that we will receive what we ask of Him. In James 1:6 the apostle says that when we ask we must not doubt, because a man who doubts is like a wave of the sea, and no one with that kind of attitude can expect to receive anything from the Lord.

Faith is absolutely crucial to our whole prayer life. In Hebrews 10:35, the writer exhorts us,

> *Do not throw away your confidence; it will be richly rewarded.*

This principle could be applied to all aspects of Christian living but particularly applies to prayer.

It is not so much the words we utter in prayer that matter in God's sight, as the condition of our hearts. Are we praying with confidence, or out of anxious necessity? Unless we are trusting in the Lord, we will not receive the reward that the writer to the Hebrews speaks of.

Those of us with unanswered prayers should examine whether there is unbelief in our hearts when we come before the Lord to pray. If we have thrown away our confidence, all we do in our Christian lives, including intercession, is going to be useless. God will not heed our requests if they are nothing but religious exercises.

In Hebrews 11:6, the writer also points out the great importance of having faith in the Lord:

> *Without faith it is impossible to please God, because anyone who comes to him must believe that he exists and that he rewards those who earnestly seek him.*

If there is no faith behind our prayer, there will be no reward either. We are not speaking here about faith in God's existence. It's possible to believe that God exists without having a relationship with Him, and the Scriptures say, *"Even the demons believe that – and shudder"* (James 2:19).

This is a matter of having faith in God's character. As it says in another translation, *"Anyone who comes to God must believe that He is"*, meaning that He is the one that He says He is. One of the Lord's names is *"the great I AM."*

As we come to enquire of the Lord, the key to our success will be whether we are trusting in His character. In other words, it is not so much what we do when we appear before God's throne that will bring us the things that we need, as our heart attitude.

In Matthew 6:6, Jesus says:

> *"But when you pray, go into your room, close the door and pray to your Father, who is unseen. Then your Father, who sees what is done in secret, will reward you."*

Again, we see that the Lord Jesus is linking prayer and reward. The very nature of prayer is that it should bring a reward.

We might wonder why the Lord should advise us to shut ourselves in our room to be alone with our Father. But as long as we are together with other people, for instance in a corporate prayer gathering, we are easily stimulated to put on a pretence. So, the Father wants us to come before Him in the secret place where our hearts are exposed and naked before Him.

The Lord wants to see how we really are and whether we have full confidence in His character, and He will reward us accordingly.

It is amazing how much unbelief we can be harbouring. In Mark 11, Jesus and His disciples were walking towards Jerusalem. As they passed by Bethany, Jesus felt hungry, and seeing a small fig tree He went to find some fruit. But when He did not find any, He cursed the tree, saying, *"May no one ever eat fruit from you again."*

Of course the disciples may have wondered what on earth was going on. It was not even the season for figs, naturally speaking, nor did anything seem to happen immediately. It was only as they came back the same way the following day that Peter noticed with great surprise that the fig tree had withered. As he pointed it out to Jesus, he exposed the unbelief in his heart.

Had he trusted fully in Jesus' character when He spoke forth the curse the previous day, Peter would have known that whatever the Lord said would be fulfilled. There would then not have been any big fuss when they discovered that the fig tree had withered away. When believers are surprised to see miracles taking place, it exposes the spirit of unbelief.

If word got around that great miracles were taking place in a particular church, you can be sure that a lot of people would make a pilgrimage there just to investigate the sensational events. However, if we had hearts of faith, we would not be so greatly surprised. Signs, wonders and healings would be seen as normal, just as they were in the days of the early Church.

The Lord's response to Peter's outburst was, *"Have faith in God."* Jesus was pointing towards the central issue of faith. It was because Peter did not have this faith that he was overcome by surprise. This phrase in the original Greek can be alternatively translated, "Have God's faith," which brings out even more of the meaning of Jesus' words.

What we need is not human faith, but that divine faith given by the Holy Spirit, which is God's very own faith. It is important to mention this distinction. If we are only exercising human faith, we will be disappointed in the long run, because human faith is eventually bound to fail.

Every human being has a portion of what could be called "natural faith." If this weren't so, we would be lying in our beds fearfully twenty-four hours a day in order to prevent anything bad from happening to us. But we rise up every morning and catch the bus or drive our cars or go to the airport to board a plane. We do all these things with some confidence that we will end up in the place that we are planning to go to.

Without natural faith, nobody would take any action. However, this is not the kind of faith that we need for prayer. To approach God for miracles, we need God's own faith. We need to have trust in God's character and in His person. We need the faith that has been born of God in our hearts through the Holy Spirit.

Jesus answered Peter:

> *"I tell you the truth, if anyone says to this mountain, 'Go, throw yourself into the sea,' and does not doubt in his heart but believes that what he says will happen, it will be done for him. Therefore I tell you, whatever you ask for in prayer, believe that you have received it, and it will be yours."*
>
> (Mark 11:23–24)

This is actually one of the most amazing promises we have in the New Testament concerning the power of prayer.

Jesus is promising that by the prayer of faith it will be possible even to move mountains. We would not normally have any need to relocate physical mountains! However, mountains in the Bible signify obstacles, and specifically satanic opposition. For those who intercede and pray in faith, there is a power that can remove these mountains, the hindrances and opposition that the enemy is trying to put in the way of God's people.

However, note that Jesus says: "[If anyone] *does not doubt in his heart but believes that what he says will happen, it will be done for him."* Again, it is not so much what you say with your mouth, it is what you believe in your heart.

Many years ago, some friends in America sent me a booklet with a very interesting title, *There is a Miracle in Your Mouth*. As I was reading this little book, I understood that the author was assuming from this verse, among others, that it is possible by confession to make things happen in the spiritual realm. Undoubtedly there is a great merit in having the right confession, but the miracle has to happen in your heart before it is expressed through your mouth.

If you do not have that Spirit-given faith in your heart, you cannot accomplish anything by issuing proclamations and confessions. A mere technique of saying words on their own will not cause things to happen. That would be pure magic. It is what is in your heart that dictates what can happen when you open your mouth.

This same principle is found in Romans 10:10, where Paul says:

> *It is with your heart that you believe and are justified, and it is with your mouth that you confess and are saved.*

Notice the combination here, and even the sequence. First, you must believe in your heart in Christ; then, you must confess with your mouth that He is Lord, and only then, you will be saved. But just opening your mouth and uttering the words, "Jesus is Lord" cannot save you. Faith is given as a seed in your heart, and as you exercise that faith through confession, the miracle of salvation will be complete.

I am not saying that confessions are not powerful and important. They are, but only if they reflect the trust already present in your heart.

We find the very same truth being underlined by the Lord Jesus in Luke 11:11–13, just after He has taught on the Lord's Prayer:

> *"Which of you fathers, if your son asks for a fish, will give him a snake instead? Or if he asks for an egg, will give him a scorpion? If you then, though you are evil, know how to give good gifts to your children, how much more will your Father in heaven give the Holy Spirit to those who ask him!"*

Once again, trust in the character of God is the key to successful prayer and intercession. If an earthly father can be trusted when it comes to giving gifts to his children, how much more can we trust that our heavenly Father would only give us good things in answer to our prayers?

Some years ago, I met a believer who for eleven years had been seeking baptism in the Holy Spirit. She was distressed that God never seemed to respond to her prayers and give her this charismatic experience. As a mature woman of God she couldn't understand why she had so much difficulty in receiving the power of the Spirit when all around her in our meetings, newly saved people seemed to be able to receive that gift almost automatically. And she asked whether God had something against her.

Of course, I assured her that God was in no way prejudiced against her. But I asked what she really was expecting in her heart when she came before the Lord. She responded immediately that she certainly did not want to receive in the way "those Pentecostals" did. By her reply I realized that it was because of her mistrust that this sister had not been able to receive the promised gift. She actually feared that God would give her something bad when she prayed for the Holy Spirit.

A suspicious, fearful or unbelieving heart will always prevent us from receiving anything from the Lord. The question is whether we dare believe that God is our Father, that He is entirely trustworthy, and that He would never ever give us anything wrong.

In James 5 we find how important faith is to the whole life of prayer. Here the apostle speaks about Elijah, that he was a man with a nature like ours, and he prayed earnestly that it would not rain, and it did not rain on the land for three years and six months. Then Elijah prayed again, and the heaven gave rain and the earth produced its fruit. In verse 16, James says,

The prayer of a righteous man is powerful and effective.

James is pointing out that Elijah was just an ordinary human being like us, yet he was able to break through in prayer to the extent that it did not rain in Israel for three years and six months, and then once again by his prayer, to make it rain again.

We need to take this amazing truth to our hearts. If Elijah was able to enter into such a position before God, then we can also. In Old Testament times people were more limited than we are now, and yet Elijah influenced his entire nation with his prayers. Because of our unbelief, we wouldn't dare to compare ourselves with a man like Elijah, or dream of doing the same great deeds. Yet James stresses that we have the same possibilities as Elijah did in this realm of prayer.

The apostle James is a very straightforward person who says things the way they are. In chapter 5, he writes:

> *Is any one of you in trouble? He should pray. Is anyone happy? Let him sing songs of praise. Is any one of you sick? He should call the elders of the church to pray over him and anoint him with oil in the name of the Lord. And the prayer offered in faith will make the sick person well; the Lord will raise him up. If he has sinned, he will be forgiven. Therefore confess your sins to each other and pray for each other so that you may be healed. The prayer of a righteous man is powerful and effective.*
>
> (James 5:13–16)

These verses seem to give godly counsel to all categories of people in the local church. *"Is any one of you in trouble?"* James asks to begin with, and instructs, *"You should pray."* This is actually a very simple, and yet most revolutionary answer.

When people go through suffering and hardships, their reaction is often to seek counsel with their pastor or elders. There is nothing wrong with that, but if they prayed immediately they would be able to come through their difficulties by communicating directly with the Lord.

In this way, they would certainly ease the burden on the leadership of the local church. Also, these people would quickly begin to grow in their spiritual lives. We are not meant to lean so heavily upon mediators in our relationship with the Lord. This is actually an Old Testament concept. Under the New Covenant, all believers have the right to come before God's throne and present their needs.

Then, there is another category of people in the church: those who are happy. James says they should sing songs of praise. So if things are going well for us and we are in a good mood, we should not forget to turn it all into worship and thanksgiving. This is a way of assuring our well-being in the Lord and keeping our hearts lifted. We are not to be happy for the sake of being happy. God wants our happiness to bring glory to His name, as a testimony of His great faithfulness.

The third category James deals with in these verses is those who are sick. Again, his answer seems very simple: if we are sick, we should call the elders of the church to pray over us, anointing us with oil in the name of the Lord. The prayer of faith will bring healing and the Lord will raise us up.

Sometimes those who are sick will try to find some person with a special gift of healing, perhaps even travelling a long distance to seek the help of a "faith healer." It is true that God has given special gifts to certain Christians for the blessing of the Church. But the normal procedure when people are sick in the church is simply to seek prayer and anointing from the local elders. And the Lord promises that He will raise up the sick ones.

Again our lack of faith is an obstacle. Church members often hesitate to be prayed for by their own local elders, because they know them so very well. They are aware of their weaknesses or lack of gifting in particular areas, and so they have no expectation that God will move through their prayers. That attitude is again a manifestation of the spirit of unbelief.

In reality, it has nothing to do with the elders whether a sick person will be healed or not. The elders are only instrumental in this process. Neither does the oil poured out on the sick magically cause healing. It is a matter of faith in the heart of the sick person, and in those praying. Faith will bring a great breakthrough but without faith, the anointing will be nothing more than religious tradition, which will not bring anything along with it.

It is said that early in his ministry the well-known Chinese Bible teacher, Watchman Nee, learned this lesson of trusting in the Lord and in the simple ordinances of His Word. Brother Nee had a weak bodily constitution and was often ill during his travels to spread the gospel across China. He would, however, very often experience the Lord's sovereign touch when he turned to Him in prayer. But one day something unusual happened.

On one of his journeys, Watchman Nee came to a small village where he was supposed to meet with the local believers. However, once he arrived, he became unwell and had to stay in bed. And as he was lying there, he cried out to the Lord for His touch once again, to heal him and raise him up so that he could be ready for ministry when the people came to the house for the evening service. But this time the Lord clearly answered his request by this word, *"Is anyone of you sick? He should call the elders of the church."*

Brother Nee was very surprised and asked why he should bother to call the elders when the Lord had so many times directly intervened to heal him. But as he kept renewing his request for healing, the same word came back to him, *"Is anyone of you sick? He should call the elders of the church."*

In the course of his prayers, Brother Nee complained to the Lord that these elders were actually newly saved. All of them were poor, illiterate fishermen, and so nothing special could be expected of them spiritually. But the Lord replied by the same word, *"Is anyone of you sick? He should call the elders of the church."*

So, finally, Watchman Nee sent for the elders, who came after work into the bedroom, still smelling of fish. He brought them his request to be prayed for and anointed with oil according to James 5, but the leading elder said, "We cannot read, so we don't know exactly what is written in James 5. Would you please read it out loud for us?" Brother Nee read the text, and the leading elder turned to the wife of the house and asked, "Do you have any oil in the house?" She said, "Yes, but it is only fish oil." The elder was satisfied, saying, "Oil is oil," so she brought out a big bottle of fish oil.

This simple man opened the bottle and poured it all over Brother Nee in his bed, and it was said that Watchman Nee was stinking from fish oil for several weeks afterwards. The elders put their hands upon him and prayed and then left the place. And quickly afterwards, Brother Nee stood up completely healed and was able to continue with his ministry.

This is an example of the principle of Hebrews 10:35:

> Do not throw away your confidence; it will be richly rewarded.

We don't have to learn how to formulate our prayers so that they might impress the good Lord in heaven. If we are going to break through in intercession, we need to confess our spirit of unbelief and have our hearts cleansed. Then we can once again return to simply trusting in the character of God, and in the truth and purity of His own Word.

Discussion questions

1. What matters most as we come before the Lord in prayer?

2. How do we demonstrate faith in God's character and in His Word?

3. Which things expose a spirit of unbelief in our hearts?

4. How does "God's own faith" differ from natural faith?

5. Is anything hindering you from receiving from God?

Power Tools
for Prayer

In the New Testament, there are at least five different types of prayer mentioned. Four of them we find in 1 Timothy 2:1, where Paul says:

> I urge, then, first of all, that requests, prayers, intercession and thanksgiving be made for everyone.

A further type of prayer is found in Ephesians 6 and is generally called spiritual warfare. This is not the topic of this book but I do believe that the term "spiritual warfare" is not a very good choice of phrase. This term actually originated in the occult movements which for decades have been issuing curses primarily against the Church and Christian leaders. I would much prefer the term "prayer warfare."

There is no proper confrontation with the powers of darkness except through the ministry of prayer. And prayer always means that we focus on the Lord and that we appeal to the Lord. Even our warfare against the powers of darkness goes through the Lord and has to come before the throne. And so, in a way, we are not the ones doing the warfare, the Lord is the one who is coming against the enemy in response to our prayers.

The whole chapter of Ephesians 6 shows us clearly how the Church's conflict with the powers of darkness and our use of the whole armour of God can only be conducted in the context of prayer. That is why "prayer warfare" is a much more appropriate name for the nature of the spiritual battle that we are in.

Some have majored on spiritual warfare, thinking that we can solve all our problems by just cutting off the enemy, but this is far from the case. In 1 Timothy 2:1, Paul mentions four different kinds of prayer that are available to the Church. Let us use all the tools that God has given us rather than being one-sided. To be complete in our intercessory ministry we need to practise all five disciplines of prayer mentioned in Scripture.

1. Requests

Paul mentions "requests" as the first type of prayer. Requests, or "supplications," as they are termed in other translations of the Bible, simply mean calling upon the Lord. This does not necessarily describe a very eloquent utterance. Nor does it imply that those who making requests or supplications necessarily have full understanding of the situation for which they are praying, or of God's will. Supplication is simply the outcry of people in a desperate situation of need.

Some people today do not believe that there is a need for this kind of prayer. They assert that we are able to accomplish everything through proclamations of faith and spiritual warfare. Yet supplication may be the most powerful type of prayer found in the whole Bible, as we have scriptural evidence that it greatly moves the heart of the Father.

It was actually supplication that delivered the people of Israel from their situation of bondage in Egypt. We remember that through his slave masters, Pharaoh terrorized and tyrannized God's people more and more. When it became quite unbearable, the people began to cry to the Lord, and we read in Exodus 2:23–25:

> *During that long period, the king of Egypt died. The Israelites groaned in their slavery and cried out, and their cry for help because of their slavery went up to God. God heard their groaning and he remembered his covenant with Abraham, with Isaac and with Jacob. So God looked on the Israelites and was concerned about them.*

The tremendous cry for mercy coming from the hearts of God's people made the Lord remember His covenant with Abraham, Isaac, and Jacob. It was out of that strong supplication that God took action, calling Moses at the burning bush in the wilderness and sending him to Egypt to deliver his fellow Israelites from their affliction.

In every kind of revival we have seen in the history of the Church, this kind of supplication has played a very significant role. So, as we learn to just cry out to God for the needs of our Church and nation, we will be able to touch His heart in a very special way.

We must never forget that God primarily sees Himself as our Father, and as a father, He has a very tender heart. The strongest part of God's character is that of mercy. He is a holy, righteous and faithful God, but beyond all these other qualities, He is a God of mercy. That is our great opportunity when we think about the situation we are in, within the Church and within the nation. We can actually call upon this aspect of His nature.

When we appeal to God's mercy, even if we are still in rebellion, God will be touched. Despite the fact that stiff-necked people do not deserve salvation, deliverance, or revival, when God's people are crying out their hearts before Him, He will respond and pour out His grace and mercy upon the whole situation.

There is great power in supplication, as we see also in the New Testament. In Romans 10:11–13, Paul writes:

> *As the Scripture says, "Anyone who trusts in him will never be put to shame." For there is no difference between Jew and Gentile – the same Lord is Lord of all and richly blesses all who call on him, for, "Everyone who calls on the name of the Lord will be saved."*

This is truly the way of salvation: Whoever calls on the name of the Lord will be saved. Before your own conversion, how much did you know about the Lord, His law, and about principles of Christian living? Most of us did not know God's statutes and were caught in sin, but because we were in desperate need we called upon the name of the Lord. And what happened? We were saved. What a tremendous power there is in supplication!

I believe that supplication or requests are the most powerful factor in producing a revival. It is just as with the people of Israel in Egypt. Once we reach the point of being no longer able to tolerate what is going on, we begin to call upon the name of the Lord for help. When we are fed up with our own deadness, with the deadness of the

Church, and the abundance of sin in the people amongst whom we live, we will cry out our desperate need to heaven.

When we do so, we see the Lord respond with great power. Hence there is a great need for this kind of prayer in the ministry of intercession today.

2. Prayers of petition

The second type of prayer listed by Paul in 1 Timothy 2:1 is called simply "prayers" in the New International Version, but in other translations it is termed "prayers of petition." There is a very concrete way in which God wants us to put our requests before Him. So often in our "prayers," we are just telling the Lord stories, quoting scriptures, or airing our different theological views instead of really asking Him for what we need.

If you go to a typical prayer meeting today, it can be like a religious chat show! Sometimes people are just using the time to exhibit their own spirituality. Some are all over the place asking God for this, that and the other, but with nothing really burning in their hearts. Others are showing off their Bible knowledge to those present, without making any specific request of the Lord.

God wants us to know that prayer is asking of Him specific things, and as we do this, we need to expect Him to give us what we pray for.

I once conducted an experiment at a time when the Lord was teaching me the nature of real prayer. As the pastor, I would stand in the doorway to greet people as they left the church after a meeting. But one particular evening, I asked every brother and sister who had participated in the prayer meeting to tell me what he or she had specifically asked the Lord for that night.

It was a shocking experience, and I am not sure that I would ever like to repeat it. Most of the people did not have a clue as to what they had asked God for that evening; others were confused and without a sense of direction.

I realized that God will not have us use our prayer meetings as "religious performances." He wants us to come before His face with clear and specific requests. After all, the Lord Jesus taught us that whatever we ask, His Father in heaven will give to us. God delights to hear specifically from His children.

We have to make sure when starting to pray that we know what we really want from God for our own individual lives, and for the Church, and also for our nation. It is part of the discipline of petitioning the Lord.

3. Intercession

Intercession is the third type of prayer mentioned in 1 Timothy 2:1 and we have already discussed some of its unique qualities.

Intercession is a deeper form of prayer, requiring a much stronger commitment from the one who prays. Ordinary prayer can be offered up for people and situations at a distance, so to speak, but if we desire to truly intercede, we need to identify with those for whom we are praying.

Identification is perhaps what most distinguishes true intercession. We can offer up prayers for people and situations all the time, without really affecting our own personal situation. But with intercession, this is no longer enough. We cannot remain in our own secure position.

We need to move from where we are and to take the place of the people for whom we are interceding. When we identify with those who are in deep trouble and need, we take upon ourselves their burdens.

Rees Howells, the great intercessor from Wales, was a remarkable man in this respect. The biography, *Intercessor*, speaks about the way he identified with some of the people for whom he was praying.

In the particular city where he was living, there was a man of violence, a wild vagabond. This man was notorious for disrupting church services and for other bad behaviour. The believers in the city were deeply concerned and were spending much time in prayer for the man.

Rees Howells took on a special burden to intercede for this troubled person. As soon as he started praying, the Holy Spirit impressed upon his heart the need to identify with the man's desperate situation in a very physical way.

The man was living in the slum; he was addicted to alcohol, never washed and grew an untidy beard. And the Spirit guided Rees Howells to go and live together with this man for some time in order to understand his need and also to show him the love of God.

So, Rees Howells left his pleasant, secure home. Although he did not take on the man's drinking or hygiene habits, he decided to stay in the same area as this poor man and thereby identify with his situation, while crying out to the Lord on his behalf.

After some time, the burden on Rees Howell for this man's salvation became so strong that he started feeling that if God would not save this sinner, he would never be able to be released from his commitment and return to his home. He actually felt the burden so intensely that it was as if it had really become a matter of his own life or death. And it was at that point that the Lord answered his prayers. In a sovereign and miraculous way, God saved and delivered this violent drunkard and made him a great testimony in the city.

This is the true heart of intercession. We need to remember how the Lord Jesus did exactly that. Jesus could have stayed in glory and offered up the most eloquent and righteous prayers for our salvation, but in His love the Son of God left heaven and came down to identify completely with our sorrows, sins and all of our humanity. In every way He was tempted, though without sin, and from that position that Jesus was able to intercede for our salvation.

When some years ago, the Lord put upon my heart to pray especially for the Jewish people to be released from the Communist Soviet Union, I felt after a while that I needed to go and see them for myself. So I joined up with a team on a prayer tour to some of the major Jewish communities in the former Soviet Union. While on that trip I began to realize what it means to intercede for a group of people.

As we met some of the Jews in Moscow, Odessa and other places, we sensed the great oppression and persecution they were living under. Praying for them there was quite another thing from just offering up prayers on their behalf while staying safely in our own countries.

I remember especially in the city of Volgograd how the Lord put us in touch with a Jewish man who brought us to the flat of his brother and sister-in-law. While there, we were able to share about Israel and the return of the Jewish people from the four corners of the earth to the ancient land of their forefathers. These people were so taken by that prospect that we had to spend several extra hours explaining everything to them.

After we left their flat, we were waiting in the car to be taken back to the hotel. Suddenly the Jewish man came running down the stairs, opened the back door of the car where I was sitting, and with tears running down his face, said with a heart full of desire, "Please come back and help us to return to Israel."

I remember that I began to weep as well. When I returned from the Soviet Union and continued praying, I could picture this tearful face as if in a vision, and hear that voice begging, "Come back and help us to get out of here." That made such a difference to my prayer life and my commitment to intercede for the Jews to be released from the Soviet Union.

This is what intercession is about: to identify with people in their need and to share their burden, as well as to feel some of their pain and distress in our own lives.

We need to be aware that it is possible to carry the principle of identification too far. Some Christians believe that we can confess other people's sins so that God would save these people. That is not so and cannot be found in the Word of God.

It is true that we are able to repent on behalf of the sins of other people and to plead with God for mercy, but this does not take away their personal responsibility. What it can do is to open up the way for more grace to flow, as well as buying these sinners more time so that they might eventually turn to God. But ultimately they must personally repent, confess, and ask for forgiveness.

We know that Moses identified with the people of Israel in their rebellion against God. He confessed sins on their behalf, and asked for mercy. The Lord gave extra grace so as to not destroy the people, but to give them extended opportunities to turn away from their wicked ways.

Daniel also identified with the people of Israel as he confessed his sins and the sins of his people. By doing so he caused God to have mercy on them in their Babylonian captivity, opening the way for them to be released and led back to the land of Israel.

When we are standing in the gap for our people and repenting on their behalf, we do not imagine that God would take that as a substitute for their own involvement. What we are doing is asking God for a visitation; we are asking in His grace to send revival instead of judgment and destruction upon our people.

Such identification touches God's heart and consequently has great power. As when Moses interceded for Israel, the Lord was long-suffering and promised to delay the reckoning that had to be made for the sins of the people. He gave them extra opportunity to turn away from their rebellion and turn back to Him.

4. Thanksgiving

The fourth type of prayer mentioned here is thanksgiving. Giving thanks is, of course, a part of worship, and worship plays an important role in intercession. But as it is expressed here, it has a particular meaning.

Thanksgiving is evidence of our faith in the Lord, as we see in the New Testament. This is because when we give thanks in every situation we honour and glorify God. When we intercede for very grave problems, we must always remember that God is altogether righteous.

The dreadful situations we see in our world are never God's fault or design. Therefore in our prayers we need to give God his place of supremacy, honour His name and beware of ever blaming Him for what may be going on.

Thanksgiving is a powerful type of prayer that enables the Lord to respond to our prayers with pleasure and favour. There is actually no situation in which we ought not to lift up the holy name of God and thank Him for being the wonderful Father that He is.

Discussion questions

1. Why might "prayer warfare" be a better term than "spiritual warfare"?

2. What evidence do we have that requests or supplications greatly move the heart of the Father?

3. Why is it important to ask, or petition, the Lord specifically for things?

4. What does it mean to identify with people in our intercession?

5. How is thanksgiving important in our prayer lives? Are you doing it enough?

The Purpose of Intercession

In thinking about why the Lord is calling us to intercede, we need to understand what the real purpose is of this tremendously important ministry.

To pray as a mere religious habit is meaningless. It makes little sense to separate the ministry of intercession from the overall purposes of God. Intercessors are not supposed to be a special group of people who are only concentrating on prayer. We have to align ourselves with other ministries in the Body of Christ and realize what God is doing universally.

The overall purpose of the work of the Church is to bring in the Kingdom of God. We do not pray for our own personal satisfaction, we pray in order to prosper God's purposes on earth.

One of the chief goals for intercessory prayer is to produce a spiritual revival in our society. When Paul exhorts us to pray for everyone, including kings and all who are in authority, he is motivated by the desperate need for revival.

The prayer ministry of the Church has a very positive focus. It is not chiefly to battle against sin and the negative things in the world. Its ultimate purpose is to open up the way for an outpouring of the Holy Spirit that will revive the Church and bring multitudes of people into the Kingdom of God.

In 1 Timothy 2, the apostle Paul instructs the Church to pray these different kinds of prayer for all people. Notice that Paul begins by saying *"first of all."* This is a clear priority in the work of the Church.

Paul's two letters to his young friend and co-worker Timothy are full of vital instructions for the work and service of the local church. He covers many subjects, such as men and women in the church, the qualifications for the ministry of being elders and deacons, warnings against the coming of a great apostasy, the care for widows, and ministry towards the poor and needy.

These are all important, but the very first on the list deals with prayer. Paul is saying that the chief ministry of the local church is the fourfold ministry of prayer. Our foremost call is to pray, not just for the local affairs of the church, but for all people everywhere and especially those in authority.

If the Church really obeyed this exhortation, I am convinced that the situation in our nations would be very different. Often we have totally forgotten that our most important calling is to be a body of prayer for revival in our local society.

Of course it is essential to pray for the Church. Yet we must put our priorities right. We are called to intercede for everyone, which means many more people than those who happen to belong to the Church. The vast majority of people are still outside the Church.

It does not seem that Paul is instructing the local church here to embrace the whole world in its prayers. His exhortation to pray for kings and all who are in authority indicates that we should be praying for all those who are part of the society in which we live.

In a narrower sense, it means to pray for our city, and in a broader sense, it means to pray for the nation under whose rule we are living. Some churches have found an effective, systematic way to fulfil this calling.

I know of a church that has divided up the people of their city into different sectors and allotted prayer assignments to different prayer groups. One group especially prays for the mayor and the city government; another intercedes for the working community, and yet another one is praying for the children and the schools. Still another group has a special responsibility to intercede for poor people and drug addicts, and so on. When the church meets for prayer once a week, they spend about six hours together praying in groups for all these different classes of people within their city.

Because of their intercession, the members of this church have become involved in communicating with the particular groups of people that they are praying for. They have been able to establish close contacts with people such as the city authorities and have had the joy of seeing a number of people saved.

Why did the apostle Paul underline the necessity of praying for kings and all who are in authority? Many Christians draw back as soon as they hear talk about praying for governments and people in authority, because they fear we are getting involved in party politics. But that is far from our motive. The Scriptures clearly reveal that the government as an institution is something that has been established by God for the sake of our lives and security.

People in government do have an extensive influence on

those that they are ruling over, and so it matters whether those leading our cities and nations are righteous or if they are given to corruption and abuse of power.

Secondly, when we pray for those in authority we are dealing with unseen powers that lie behind our government. We know that this present world is in the hands of the evil one, who has established principalities and powers to rule on his behalf over local regions and nations. When the Church does not intercede for the government, it gives the powers of darkness free reign and influence. And this is what we have seen so clearly over the past many years.

Today, there is hardly any government in the Western world that is not deeply infiltrated by the powers of darkness. In several European countries, for instance, cabinet members are Freemasons or members of other occult or New Age movements. No wonder the continent of Europe is drifting farther and farther away from its original Christian basis. The devil has gained a foothold in so many nations, by and large because the Church is not fulfilling its role to cut off his influence and replace it with the influence of the Holy Spirit.

It is the Church in prayer that makes the difference, and that is why Paul is calling for us to pray for kings and those in authority. It is in order that *"we may live peaceful and quiet lives in all godliness and holiness. This is good, and pleases God our Saviour"* (1 Timothy 2:2–3).

Paul is speaking about peace, righteousness and reverence in human society. He is not necessarily referring to a Christian community, but a spirit of righteousness prevailing even in secular society. It is important for us to know that intercession has the power to change the spiritual climate in cities and nations. Through it we can cut off the influence of the powers of darkness and cause light to prevail in the hearts of the rulers as well as in ordinary people.

That is one aspect of revival. Revival is more than people getting converted. Of course in all revivals there has been a great harvest of people being saved. But there has also been an impact upon the whole society by the power of the Holy Spirit. When the Church is obeying the calling to intercede for our secular society, and for those who are in government, there will be a change in the moral climate. A spirit of unrighteousness, corruption and abuse of power will be replaced by a spirit of righteousness and justice.

Paul is also encouraging the Church to intercede so that we can open up a way for the gospel to be preached and received by people in secular society. He goes on to say that:

> [God] *wants all men to be saved and to come to a knowledge of the truth. For there is one God and one mediator between God and men, the man Christ Jesus, who gave himself as a ransom for all men – the testimony given in its proper time.*
>
> (1 Timothy 2:4–6)

So often in evangelism we forget that we need more than good and anointed preaching of the gospel. We also need people to be delivered from satanic oppression and deception, and to have their hearts prepared to receive the word of truth. Intercession is able to bring that about in the hearts of people in our community. Therefore, we see that whenever the Church is praying effectively it will create a thirst and hunger for God in the unsaved people all around.

Paul concludes in 1 Timothy 2:8

> *I want men everywhere to lift up holy hands in prayer,*
> *without anger or disputing.*

The aim is for a ministry of prayer in every locality where believers are worshipping without wrath and doubting. This is God's greatest desire today. The first step in conquering an area for the Kingdom of God is establishing groups of men and women who are moving in unity, who have put their relationships right so that they can pray in all holiness.

May the Lord in His mercy help us to understand this priority in the heart of God! There is no doubt in my mind that intercession is the most powerful ministry that the Church of Jesus Christ today can exercise. As we learn the principles of true intercession we will see the break-throughs we long for in the cities and nations of the world.

Discussion questions

1. What does it mean to align intercession with other
    ministries of the church?

2. How can we pray effectively for our cities?

3. Why does Paul tell us to pray for kings and those in
    authority over us?

4. How would you define revival?

5. Are you praying in unity with other believers in your
    locality? If not, how could you bring that about?

If you have enjoyed this book and would like to help us to send a copy of it and many other titles to needy pastors in developing nations, please write for further information or send your gift to:

**Sovereign World Trust
PO Box 777, Tonbridge
Kent TN11 0ZS
United Kingdom**

or to the **'Sovereign World'** distributor in your country.

Visit our website at **www.sovereign-world.com** for a full range of Sovereign World books.